WISDOM
Pearls

Moheindu
Chemjong

To my parents
Brigadier General (Retd.)
Mohan Chemjong
and Indu Chemjong

from whom I learned to
open up my mind, and
see unlimited possibilities.

Wisdom Pearls
by Moheindu Chemjong

Published by Indu Chemjong.
Production support by Spiny Babbler.
Layout and design by Manisha Maharjan.

Colour artwork and photographs by the author.
Pencil sketches by Manisha, Urvee,
Ella, Monalisha, Norbu, and Aavaneesh.

Comments, views, and opinions in this publication are that of
respective authors and may not represent the opinions and views
of the author or the publisher.

https://artrepreneur.com/p/kqdPDgiQinmduhPuj

Printed in Kathmandu

ISBN: 978-9937-2-7372-5

A few words

Wisdom Pearls is a collection of beautiful pearls of wisdom that I collected over the course of my student years. These thoughts have been taken from many books and magazines, brochures and booklets. I thank all those inspirational people who shared their wisdom with the world.

I learned note-taking as a student and I started making notes of all the beautiful thoughts/words I could get my hands on. Whenever I feel I or anyone could do with some beautiful thoughts, I turn to these notebooks for the wisdom contained in them and share them with friends and colleagues alike.

One morning, a thought crossed my mind. Something told me to practice generosity and share these pearls of wisdom with my fellow human beings. Hence, here I come. You don't have to read the book serially. You can turn to any page any day!

Reflect on the words and think about them or read them out aloud or write them down but do enjoy the wisdom contained, and learn. You can start the same process again, some other day. I offer these pearls of wisdom to you.

Take a cup of tea, early in the morning, go through the pages and end the reading as you finish your cup of tea. Begin your day with a wisdom pearl.

Best wishes,
Moheindu

Dream Big

*I*f there was ever a time to dare, to make a difference, to embark on something worth doing, IT IS NOW. Not for any grand cause, necessarily… but for something that's your inspiration, something that's your dream.

You owe it to yourself to make your days count here. HAVE FUN. DIG DEEP. STRETCH. DREAM BIG. Know, though, that things worth doing seldom come easy. There will be good days. And there will be bad days. There will be times when you want to turn back, pack it up, and call it quits. These times tell you that you are pushing yourself and that you are not afraid to learn by trying.

PERSIST. Because with an idea, determination and the right tools, you can do great things. Let your instincts, your intellect and your heart guide you.

TRUST. Believe in the incredible power of the human mind. Of doing something that makes a difference. Of working hard. Of laughing and hoping. Of lazy afternoons. Of lasting friends. Of all the things that will cross your path this year.

The start of something new brings the hope of something great. ANYTHING IS POSSIBLE. There is only one you. And you will pass this way only once. Do it right.

So, go on… DREAM BIG!

You are:
1. true
2. noble
3. right
4. pure
5. lovely
6. admirable

Learn to be silent. Let your
quiet mind listen and absorb.
- Pythagoras

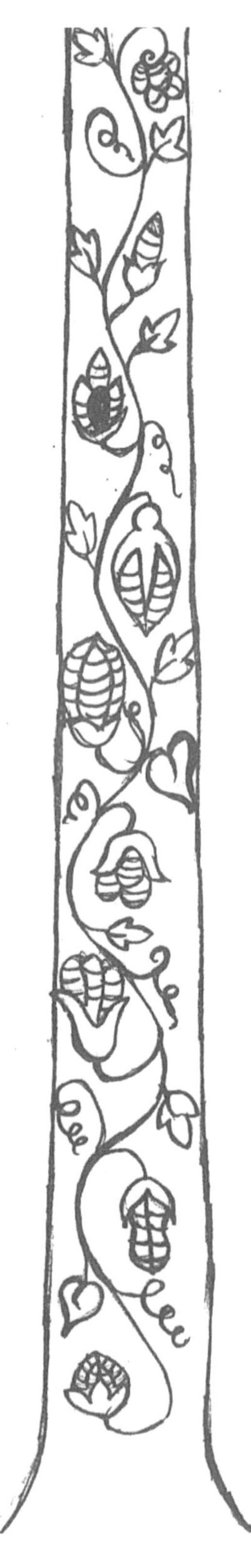

Invictus

Out of the night that covers me,
Black as the pit from pole to pole,
I thank whatever gods may be
For my unconquerable soul.

In the fell clutch of circumstance
I have not winced nor cried aloud.
Under the bludgeonings of chance
My head is bloody, but unbowed.

Beyond this place of wrath and tears
Looms but the horror of the shade,
And yet the menace of the years
Finds, and shall find, me unafraid.

It matters not how strait the gate,
How charged with punishments the scroll.
I am the master of my fate:
I am the captain of my soul.

- William Ernest Henley

"Don't wait for good things to happen to you. If you go out and make some good things happen, you will fill the world with hope, you will fill yourself with hope."

-Barack Obama

I found this last letter in an old Newsweek magazine and it deeply touched my heart... written by a soldier who lost his life in the war.

PATRIOTISM

Well, if you are reading this, I guess this deployment was a one way trip. I just have a few things to ask. Please don't be mad at the marine corps. It was my choice to join and come here. I honestly believe this is what I was meant to do. I don't care what the media says, we are making a difference here.

KNOW THAT I DID NOT DIE FOR SOME WORTHLESS CAUSE. I died in memory of all those who gave their lives before me. We are fighting for those who can't fight for themselves. And I think that is the right thing to do. Not all the people here are bad, so please don't fill your hearts with anger and hate.

When I was a kid, my dad gave me a Louis L'Amour book. On the back of the book were quotes from all his books. One that really stuck in my head and I tried to live by since the day I read it, was on Courage. "Whenever there was trouble, you never had to look back to see if he was there, you knew damn well he was." I hope I lived up to that.

Another thing I ask is that, at my funeral, the marine corps hymn, "Amazing Grace", is played with bagpipes. Nothing sounds better than bagpipes playing, "Amazing Grace." I know that I have not been the best son, brother, friend or boyfriend and I'm sorry.

If you can find it in your heart, forgive me. Ashley can keep my Hi5 if he wants. Another thing I ask is at least one of you travel to see the world. Do the things I never got to do. It is really hard writing this.

There's so much I want to say, I'm at a loss for words. Just know that I have God in my life in a better place and marines guard the streets to Heaven. Who else would God trust? Tell... that I could not have had better friends. Tell... that I'm sorry and I'm stupid. I really did love her. To my family I love you all.

Just know that I made it to Heaven before you and will see you all again. Until we meet again my heart, soul and love are with you.

$\mathcal{S}$ome pearls of wisdom for you...

- The path to glory is always rugged.

- A short saying often contains much wisdom.
  - Sophocles

- It does not matter how slowly you go as long
  as you do not stop.
  - Confucius

- A funny thing about life, if you refuse to accept
  anything but the best, you will get it.

- If you risk nothing, then you risk everything.
  - Geena Davis

- Having recognized that all difficulties come to teach you,
  you are wise, and free to fly like an angel.

- Do a little more each day than you think you possibly can.

- You are a soul who has full control over your mind and the
  thoughts you create. No one can make you unhappy.

- Reading is a means of thinking with another person's mind;
  it forces you to stretch your own.
  - Charles Scribner, Jr.

- With pure thoughts you are able to forgive and forget, and
  fly towards the loving light of God.

- Be the master of your thoughts and create a beautiful life.

- People may doubt what you say, but they will always believe
  what you do.

The Power of 'As If'

Acting or behaving as if you were
the wise, calm, creative or confident
person you want to be is magically
effective. It is highly motivating and
energizing, it also sends out powerful
signals to you as well as to others about
the direction in which you are heading.

Your mind
works/thinks
in pictures.
Visualize the
outcomes
you want!

Wisdom Pearls

- The best way to cheer yourself up is to try to cheer somebody else.
  - Mark Twain

- When the character of a man is not clear to you, look at his friends.
  - Japanese Proverb

- You may be disappointed if your fail, but you're doomed if you don't try.
  - Beverly Sills

- In the middle of difficulty, lies opportunity.
  - Albert Einstein

- Think highly of yourself for the world takes you at your own estimate.
  - Unknown

- Either write something worth reading or do something worth writing.
  - Benjamin Franklin

- You are educated when you have the ability to listen to almost anything without losing your temper or self-confidence.
  - Robert Frost

- Worrying is like the rocking chair, it gives you something to do but it gets you nowhere.
  - Glen Turner

- Motivation will almost always beat mere talent.
  - Norman R. Augustine

- It's never too late to be what you might have been.
  - George Eliot

Think, Plan... and Play

When you are thinking about your life, don't pay attention only to your sufferings or your mistakes or the things that have gone wrong or even the behaviours you believed you needed to "work out."

Life is also for living. Life is abundantly and overwhelmingly for living!

Pay attention to your triumphs, your joys, your energy, vigor, your daydreams, exuberance, excessiveness; your capacity to sing in the kitchen or dance naked under the stars.

Relish your choice to cook, paint or write for the sheer pleasure of it, to make love, laugh loudly, walk vigorously; to re-read a favourite novel or poem or see a movie on a wet afternoon; to eat with pleasure; to talk for an hour with a darling friend on the other side of the world; to tell people how much you love them; to gaze into the day as the sun rises or as the stars emerge, or to sit under a tree smelling sweet earth and thinking about absolutely nothing at all.

Advice to beloved daughters...

From this lovely book *"Things I Want My Daughters to Know"* by Alexandra Stoddard

- The world stands aside to let anyone pass who knows where he is going.
  - David Starr Jordan

- A man can succeed at almost anything for which he has unlimited enthusiasm.
  - Thomas A. Edison

- Face the thing that seems overwhelming and you will be surprised your fear will melt away.
  - Dale Carnegie

- Saints are sinners who believe in God and keep trying.
  - Anonymous

- Time is like a river of fleeting events and its current is strong.
  - Marcus Aurelius

- The harder I work, the better I plan, the luckier I get.
  - Anonymous

- Life is too short to be little.
  - Benjamin Disraeli

- Success comes from mastering fundamentals, developing physical and mental toughness, hard work, and making the second effort.
  - Vince Lombardi

- The greatest discovery of my generation is that a human being can alter his life by altering his attitudes.
  - William James

- The ability to get along with and motivate people is life's greatest ability.
  - Dale Carnegie

Abraham Lincoln's Letter to his son's Head Master

Respected Teacher,

My son will have to learn I know that all men are not just, all men are not true. But teach him also that for every scoundrel there is a hero; that for every selfish politician, there is a dedicated leader. Teach him that for every enemy there is a friend.

It will take time, I know; but teach him, if you can, that a dollar earned is far more valuable than five found. Teach him to learn to lose and also to enjoy winning. Steer him away from envy, if you can. Teach him the secret of quiet laughter. Let him learn early that the bullies are the easiest to lick. Teach him, if you can, the wonder of books, but also give him quiet time to ponder over the eternal mystery of birds in the sky, bees in the sun, and flowers on a green hill-side.

In school teach him it is far more honourable to fail than to cheat. Teach him to have faith in his own ideas, even if everyone tells him they are wrong. Teach him to be gentle with gentle people and tough with the tough. Try to give my son the strength not to follow the crowd when everyone is getting on the band-wagon.

Teach him to listen to all men but teach him also to filter all he hears on a screen of truth and take only the good that comes through. Teach him, if you can, how to laugh when he is sad. Teach him there is no shame in tears. Teach him to scoff at cynics and to beware of too much sweetness. Teach him to sell his brawn and brain to the highest bidders; but never to put a price tag on his heart and soul.

Teach him to close his ears to a howling mob... and to stand and fight if he thinks he's right. Treat him gently; but do not cuddle him because only the test of fire makes fine steel. Let him have the courage to be impatient, let him have the patience to be brave. Teach him always to have sublime faith in himself because then he will always have sublime faith in mankind.

This is a big order; but see what you can do. He is such a fine little fellow, my son.

Abraham Lincoln

Promise Yourself

- Promise yourself that you will be so strong that nothing can disturb your peace of mind.

- Promise yourself that you will make all your friends feel that there is something in them.

- Promise yourself that you will think only the best, expect only the best and to work for only the best.

- Promise yourself that you will give so much time to the improvement of others that you will have no time to criticize them.

- Promise yourself that you will be too large for worry, too noble for anger, too strong for fear, too happy to live in the past.

- Promise yourself that you will wear a cheerful countenance at all times and give every living creature you meet a smile.

- Promise yourself that that you will forget the mistakes of the past and press on to greater achievements for the future.

 Freedom

Choose freedom: cast away the gravity of doubt
For this is the time that cannot come again.
Now is the only time to spread the wings
To take us from the fear that anchors
And the need that bars the prisons of life.
To be free, look sharp
To be sharp, hear clearly
Freedom can be found in any place
There is no place to find
No words to say.
Nothing to learn but faith and bravery.
Gather freedom and fly within the unbound soul.
Be free within the walls.

\- Annie Otness

Some pearls of wisdom for you...

- Paint the walls of your mind with many beautiful pictures.
  - William Phelps

- If we are basically positive in attitude, we will attract and create people, situations, and events which confirm our positive expectations.
  - Shaladi Gawari

- Dreams that do come true can be as unsettling as those that don't.
  - Brett Butler

- Too much of a good thing can be wonderful.
  - Mae West

- I do not try to dance better than anyone else. I only try to dance better than myself.
  - Mikhail Baryshnikov

- Develop interest in life as you see it; in people, things, literature, music – the world is so rich, simply throbbing with rich treasures, beautiful souls and interesting people. Forget yourself.
  - Henry Miller

- Music washes away from the soul the dust of everyday life.
  - Auerboch Berthold

"Say No to No"

Newsweek, Advertisement of Shell

Isn't it high time someone got negative about negativity? Yes, it is. Look around. The world is full of things that according to nay-sayers, should never have happened.

"Impossible."

"Impractical."

"No."

And yet "Yes."

Yes, continents have been found. Yes, men have played golf on the Moon. Yes, straw is being turned into biofuel to power cars. Yes, yes, yes. What does it take to turn "No" into "Yes"? Curiosity. An open mind. A willingness to take risks. And, when the problem seems most insolvable, when the challenge is the hardest, when everyone also is shaking their heads, say:

"Let's go".

Work

- Why do we work? We work to build a better world.
- The individual entrepreneur today is often far more competitive than the big corporation.
- We have a proven antidote to war: free trade.
- Success in business depends largely on your adapting skills – the ability with which you learn new things.

From a book by Stephanie Dowrick

Paid to Work

How you spend your working hours, how you make decisions, how you allow yourself to be shaped by work and how you in turn shape the work you do will profoundly affect your overall sense of well-being. Your workplace offers unique opportunities to identify and refine your values:

- You have to learn to get along with a wide range of people, some of whom you may not especially like.

- You have to learn how to compromise, postpone gratification, resolve conflicts, take criticism and cope with disappointments and injustices.

- You have to get on with work whether or not you feel like it.

- You have to be able to support other people and meet a variety of expectations.

- You have to test your creativity, flexibility, resilience and persistence.

Being equally alert, alive and true to yourself at home and work is an increasing challenge, but few contemporary challenges deserve more attention or are more worthwhile.

Traits of a Good Employee

A good employee:
- is loyal and committed.
- always attempts to see things from the company's point of view.
- shares company goals and priorities.
- is flexible.
- is dependable, when assigned a responsibility, no one has to double check to make sure it's completed.
- doesn't hide problems.
- adapts to boss's styles.
- takes initiative and follows through.
- is self-motivated.
- knows when to ask for help.
- along with voicing complaints, presents solutions.
- is a team player.

Workplace Values in Practice 

<u>Value people:</u>

- See other people as people, not as opportunities, competitors or nuisance.

- Look people in the eye. Let them see you.

- Offer respect unconditionally.

- Practice the Golden Rule: Behave towards other people as you want them to behave towards you.

- Never get other people to do your dirty work.

- Be a constant source of support and encouragement for others.

<u>Value constructive behaviour:</u>

- Recognize the emotional trail you are leaving behind.

- Talk less, listen more.

- Walk the second mile. Do more than that is absolutely required.

- Never miss an opportunity to be generous.

- Value work as a place to give service while earning a living.

- Be solution, not problem focused.

- Accept that when someone disagrees with you, they may not be wrong.

- Hear all sides before judging.

- When you observe problems, speak up constructively than destructively.

Presentations: Reducing anxiety.
Push past the fear. Go for it!

Before the presentation:

- Prepare, prepare, prepare.

- Know much more than you'll ever say.

- Memorize the first and last two minutes
  of your presentation.

- Arrive early and mingle with the
  audience as they arrive.

- In the few minutes before you go on:

  - Breathe in calmness, breathe out anxiety. Yawn.
  - Visualize your audience enthusiastically responding.

- Remember your audience is there to hear the
  message, not stare at you. Focus on the message.
  Pace if you need to. Your body may need to move.

- Practice, practice, practice.

During the presentation:

- Remember to smile. It relaxes you and the audience:

  - Pick out 3 or 4 friendly faces in the audience and
    look at them when you're speaking.

- Handling a hostile audience:

  - Report or paraphrase questions in a more
    positive way. This gives you time to think.
  - As you respond, gradually shift your body language
    and eye contact away from the hostile questioner.

Work Your Way to Success

Norah Webster laboured 36 years writing his dictionary; Adam Clark spent 40 years writing his commentary on the scriptures; John Milton rose at 4 o'clock every morning in order to have sufficient time to compose and rewrite his poetry; Gibbon spent 26 years on his book, *The Decline and Fall of the Roman Empire* which stands as a monument of careful work; Bryant rewrote one of his poetic masterpieces 100 times before publication just to attain complete beauty and perfection of expression and it took Sir Issac Pitman 15 years working ten hours a day to perfect the shorthand system. These eminent men have proved that it is better to wear out than to rust out.

If we do not make an effort, we cannot succeed in life. Could an athlete hope to win the race without effort? Could a champion hope to win if he was not prepared to toil for it? It is true that modern civilization has taken away the sweat of scrubbing clothes, the aeroplanes - tedious journeys by ships or trains.

God expects us to work, that is the reason why He left oil in deep rocks, electricity in the clouds and atoms, left rivers without bridges and mountains without paths. He left books unwritten, cities unbuilt and nations unplanned. On his part, man understood the fact. If not, he would not have taken the trouble of scaling the snow-capped Everest, or sailing solo across the mighty Atlantic or exploring the Polar Regions.

As human beings, we should not lead a life of languor; we have to remember the fact that there is no substitute for hard work.

Tears, blood and sweat are part and parcel of great achievements and accomplishments. Nobody knows this better than the self-sacrificing parents, the devoted artist, the active social worker and the struggling writer. All pay a price for whatever they may accomplish. Sleepless nights and the dull ache of loneliness are part of the game.

Once Fritz Kreisler was approached by an enthusiastic musician who cried, "Mr. Kreisler, I'd give my life to play as you do." Quietly he replied, "Madam, I did." Yes, the age-old maxim, "If you want to eat the kernel, you have to crack the nut," holds good even in this modern age of test-tube babies, computers and inter-continental ballistic missiles.

Man's work does not bear full fruit unless he feels satisfaction and fulfilment in it. The tragedy of the industrial revolution was that it depersonalized and degraded humanity in the factories. But today every worker should know the importance of his or her contribution so that it may give meaning to his or her life. It is our mission on earth to make the earth more humane by transforming it through work. And by his work man puts the finishing touch to creation, he improves and adorns it. Yes, only hard work can actualize our wishes and dreams.

- Anonymous

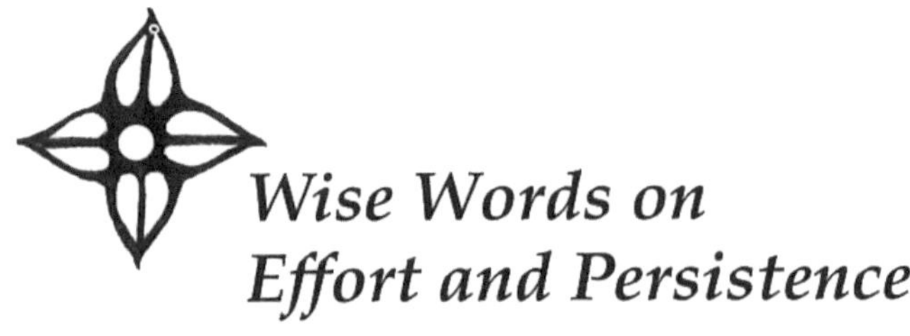

Wise Words on
Effort and Persistence

- Happiness is a state of activity.
  - Aristotle

- Never, never, never give up.
  - Winston Churchill

- The time to repair the roof is when
  the Sun is shining.
  - John F. Kennedy

- When you get to the end of your rope,
  tie a knot and hang on.
  - Franklin D. Roosevelt

- You haven't failed until you quit trying.
  - Unknown

- Success is the proper utilization of failure.
  - Unknown

- Failure is only the opportunity to begin again,
  more intelligently.
  - Henry Ford

- If the going is real easy, beware, you may be
  headed downhill.
  - Unknown

- Obstacles are those frightful things you see
  when you take your eyes off your goal.
  - Henry Ford

- I am not discouraged because every wrong
  attempt discarded is another step forward.
  - Thomas A. Edison

- Sacrifice is giving up something good
  for something better.

  - Unknown

- Our greatest glory is not in never falling,
  but in rising up every time we fail.
  - Ralph Waldo Emerson

- It is not because things are difficult that we
  do not dare, it is because we do not dare
  that they are difficult.
  - Seneca

- There is no chance, no fate, no destiny that
  can circumvent, or hinder, or control a firm
  resolve of a determined soul.
  -Ella Wheeler Wilcox

- The successful man is the average man, focused.
  - Unknown

- When you reach for the stars, you may not get one,
  but you won't come up with a handful of mud, either.
  - Leo Burnett

- Most of the important things in the world have been
  accomplished by people who have kept on trying
  when there seemed to be no hope at all.
  - Dale Carnegie

- You will come to know that what appears today
  to be sacrifice will prove instead to be the
  greatest investment that you will ever make.
  - Gorden B. Hinckley

Happiness

It gives me the greatest possible joy to imagine you sharing this list with the people you love, adding to it, making it your own, encouraging one another, applauding one another — delighting in the other's increasing happiness, as much as your own. Happiness is simply a feeling or emotion, it is a connection to the world, a realization of one's place in it.

Life is not so short but
there is always time
for courtesy.

- Ralph Waldo Emerson

You are a Source of Happiness

- You have the power to choose your own happiness. People, situations, events outside yourself will affect you. But no one can give you happiness.

- You may try to find all kinds of things outside yourself that will reassure you that you are happy or keep unhappiness at bay, but even the most substantial of them will be short lived.

- Romantic love, family, work, success, friends, status and wealth can certainly affect your well-being. Yet sometimes even in the midst of "everything" you may have a feeling that "something" is missing.

- Inner trust in who you most fundamentally are – a being of intrinsic value – makes the difference. This makes it possible for you to go on believing in happiness during the times it is out of reach or out of sight.

Emotionally:

- Think well of yourself and give yourself plenty of reasons to do so. When you let yourself down, learn something, make the change that's needed and move on.

- Pay attention to what's uplifting — and be uplifted!

- Regard your life as a gift.

- Value everything that others do for you.

- Discover and value all your strengths: intellectual, emotional, spiritual, social, creative and moral.

- Let go of resentments.

- Cultivate tolerance, patience and good humour.

- Practice forgiveness.

- Express gratitude. Find reasons to be grateful.

Socially:

- Be a peacemaker.

- Value simple pleasures.

- Give attention to and listen to others.

- Find and focus on the positive qualities in other people.

- Discover more and find out what makes others happy.

- Think and speak positively about yourself and others.

- Be the friend you would like to have.

- Practice tolerance through deeper understanding.

- Try new things or do familiar things in a fresh way.

Robin Sharma gave these gorgeous insights for a New Year. Remember every day is a new day. If you make up your mind to make a sea of change today, it is a new beginning. I wish you luck for your new beginnings. Thanks, Robin, for those pearls of wisdom:

A New Beginning

- Get fit like a proathlete.
- Surround yourself with positive, ethical people who are committed to excellence.
- Believe in your dreams (even when others laugh at them).
- Spend less, save more.
- Stay true to you deepest values and best ideals.
- Be a problem - solver not a trouble - maker.
- Commit yourself to doing great work – whether anyone notices it or not. It's one of life's best sources of happiness.
- Give more than you receive (another truth that leads to happiness).
- Under promise and over deliver.
- Wear your heart on your sleeve. When people see you're real, they'll fall in love with you.
- Eat less food.
- Demand the best from yourself.
- See everything that happens to you as an opportunity to grow (and therefore, as a precious gift).
- Use excellent words. Don't complain, gossip or be negative.

Enjoy!

Failure and Victory

I have "never failed" writing the best novel, "never failed" painting a masterpiece, "never failed" inventing that hi-tech gizmo that would change the way the world lives, "never failed" to lead my country to a brighter future.

Do you know why I have "never failed"? Simply because I have never tried. I have never tried to write that book, paint, invest or lead. To fail is okay, to never have tried is a disaster.

Victory belongs to those who take the risks and those who act. Let this not be said of you tomorrow: Ask yourself what is holding you back; all the answers are within you. I remember a poem which keeps coming back to me.

The poem follows:

Victory

You are the man who used to boast

that you'd achieve the uttermost someday

You merely wished a show

to demonstrate how much you know,

And prove the distance you can go...

Another year has just passed through

What new ideas came to you?

How many big things did you do?

Time... left twelve fresh months in your care

How many of them did you share?

With opportunity and dare

Again why were you so often missed?

We did not find you on the list of marked good

Explain the fact!

Ah no, it wasn't the chance you lacked!

As usual you failed to act!

But there are those who have not only acted

and seized every opportunity to excel, but left

imprints of their performance on the minds of

hundreds and thousands of people.

Are you one of them?

*L*uck Starts with Happiness

STOP, LOOK AND LISTEN

- Take time each day to absorb the details of your surroundings. Notice colors, designs and patterns of nature and architecture. This will heighten your sense of beauty and make you feel good.

REALISE THINGS COULD BE WORSE

- Make it a point to be thankful when good things happen to you. You'll wind up dwelling less on bad things and focus more on taking steps that improve your life.

FEEL THE BLISS

- Think about how you feel as you're experiencing what you enjoy most in life. By savouring the sensation, you allow the experience to satisfy you fully and prop up your happiness.

On God by Norman Vincent Peale...

- Put your life in the hands of God and ask him to take you and make you over.

- Are you trying to live your life without God as a partner and a close associate, one with whom you speak to and whom you believe in?

- If you have faith, nothing shall be impossible. And how do you release faith? You release it by changing the cast of your thoughts. By practicing belief rather than disbelief. If, over a long period of time, you believe that with the help of God you can overcome, you can achieve, then you will get a deep fundamental, unshakeable, unblurable picture that you can. Then your will and imagination flow together and against that power nothing negative can stand.

- Believe and your belief will in time create the fact. Beware of what you want, because there is a strong likelihood that you will get it. If you want something good and keep a primary picture of it, you will get it. It will come to you. Picturize and believe something will come true until it becomes your real desire.

- Identify yourself with success and it will come to you.

- You have to forgive if you want faith to operate in your life. You have to get all your sins out. If you have committed a sin, repent and ask God for forgiveness.

- Get rid of hate, ill, grudges, licentious and drunken sins for all these things block power.

- Go to God and ask God to cleanse your life, take away all the guilt, it will be astonishing the way power will flow through.

- Throw back the shoulders, let the heart sing, let the eyes flash, let the mind be lifted up, look upward and say to yourself, "Through the marvellous releasing power of God, nothing is impossible." Do that and live with nerve and victory and also enthusiasm, like you have never had before. Leave those old negative defects at the altar of God.

- Keep your thoughts conditioned to excitement. Never think of life as a bore. Make it alive by thinking alive. Anyone can change his thoughts if he uses discipline. If you are thinking dull, gloomy, discouraging thoughts substitute them with bright, happy, optimistic, positive thoughts. When you have accomplished all that you can, lie down and go to sleep. God is aware.

- If a sin you have committed is causing you great anxiety, get it forgiven. All you need to do right now is shut your eyes and tell God about it, telling Him that you are sorry for it and asking Him to forgive you. If you are committing any sins now, for the sake of your health and happiness and peace of mind, stop it. If you do not have the strength to stop, turn to God and tell Him you want to live under His control and let Him touch you.

- Reject the impossible, dwell on the possible. Be a possibility thinker. Consider any question by stressing the possibilities, not the impossibilities. The possible stands out like a great, shining light above the skyline of dismal clouds. "Get that bright word possibility out there among those clouds — and you will be amazed how the sky begins to clear. No matter how difficult things are, no matter how difficult, no matter how dark, keep the word, 'Possibility', firmly in your mind."

- Never accept anything but the possible; never think the impossible. There will be no more impossible in my life. I'm going to put the possibility principle to work in human affairs.

- All you need to accomplish is to have some faith. Believe it, whoever believes will have belief come to them. Miracles happen in people's lives, if they believe.

- If you allow yourself wholeheartedly and absolutely to be filled with the power of God, there is nothing that is not realizable. This is the art of successfully wishing.

- What do you want most? Practice giving that.

1. **Assume fate is on your side:**
    Believe good things happen to you all the time. If you believe you are fortunate enough most of the time, you are likely to exhibit behaviour that makes people more responsible to you.

2. **Get an emotional grip:**
    If you recognize what triggers your emotions, recognize that you tend to get upset when these emotions stir. You can take the steps to defuse or overcome them before they are expressed.

3. **Open your mind to opportunity:**
    Though you can't predict what the future has in store for you, you can improve your luck by training yourself to be more trusting of people and confident that positive outcomes will result from these encounters.

4. **Think of the world as yours:**
    You won't improve your luck sitting at home. Embrace random events that happen to you and see their potential for improving your luck. Always keep your options open and be prepared to make mistakes.

5. **Keep envy in check:**
    People who obsessively compare their lives with the lives of others often wind up feeling unlucky. In case of others, what looks ideal from the outside in reality may not be ideal for you. Stay focused on your own dreams and goals.

6. **Think like a connector:**
    The more people you know and the more likeable you are, the better your odds at becoming lucky. Most connectors are lucky because they interact with large groups of powerful people who in turn, share information and contacts just to stay in the loop. But establishing and nurturing connector relationships need not be too demanding. For example, just jotting off a birthday card or sending an email with useful information can keep you connected. If you know many different types of people, you will hear about more opportunities. Sociability, energy and openness breed luck.

7. **Find an upside to everything:**
    To feel lucky, you need a positive view of the past, as well as an optimistic view of the present. Lucky people tend to remember more of the good things that happened to them in life and block out the bad. When something bad happens, they compare the event with the worst that could have happened and realize they came out successful ahead.

 PEACE

The concept of peace in the UN has been established through the respect of the beliefs of people of all religions.

- Buddhism: World peace is accomplished if we first establish peace within our minds. This means abandoning the anger from our minds, loving one another and practicing altruism. Gautam Buddha says, "Peace comes from within. Do not seek it without."

- Hinduism: (*Basudeva Kutumbakam* or the world is one family). The more we look for wisdom, the more we become happy and free our inner spirit from worldly illusions. S. Radhakrishnan says, "Hinduism is not just a faith. It is the union of reason and intuition that cannot be defined but is only to be experienced. Evil and error are not ultimate. There is no Hell, for that means that there is a place where God is not, and there are sins which exceed His love."

- Christianity: Christianity promotes peace through benevolence, by sharing the faith with others in addition to pardoning those who break the promise.

- Islam: Islam's faith in one God and having common parents, Adam and Eve, is a great motive for all to live mutually with peace and brotherhood. Abdul Ghaffar Khan says, "The Holy Prophet Mohammed came into this world and taught us that man is a Muslim who never hurts anyone by word or deed, but who works for the benefit and happiness of God's creatures. Belief in God is to love one's fellow-men."

- Judaism: When the Messiah comes, all nations shall be cohesive in peace.

- Bahai Faith: The world must embrace collective society for the establishment of a permanent peace.

"**W**hat actions **a**re **m**ost **e**xcellent?"

* To gladden the heart of a human being,
* To feed the hungry,
* To help the afflicted,
* To lighten the sorrow of the sorrowful,
* And to remove the wrongs of the injured.

- **A**PJ **A**bdul **K**alam

Affirmations for Developing Persistence

If you get the feeling that success is not for you, try repeating the following affirmations to yourself.

1. As one day succeeds another, I develop a spirit of persistence. I will continue my efforts resolutely in spite of occasional setbacks and disappointments. I join the ranks of the undefeated.

2. I choose to continue all my efforts and enterprises. I know that patience and persistence can achieve the unbelievable. Water wears away stone and so does persistence. I will persevere until I succeed.

3. Today, I recall that many of the great achievements and discoveries of mankind have been due to persistence. I am inspired by the persistence of dedicated people like Madame Curie.

4. Today, I am nearer to my goals than ever before. I will not give up my efforts until I achieve my targets. I dedicate myself to finishing my commitments.

5. I take pride in being a person who, having put his hand to the plough, never looks back. I cultivate "stickability", the spirit which keeps on until aims have been accomplished and goals reached.

Your Values are Changing the World

- Whatever you wish there was more of, be that.

- What you want your relationships and friendships to be, be that.

- Whatever you want the world to be, be that.

- If you want there to be less fear and more love in the world, start with yourself.

- If you want there to be less stress, anxiety, depression and tension in the world, start with yourself.

- If you want the world to be a more peaceful place, fairer, more generous and compassionate, start with yourself.

Loving Yourself

I read the most beautiful book on spirituality by Ingrid Collins with marvellous pictures and wonderful words.

"You are that beautiful child. You have been sleeping through a hundred-year winter, and your castle has been neglected. Rough thorns have grown as a high, thick hedge to protect you but have also obscured your own view of your real, beautiful soul. It is now time to feel the kiss that awakens you to your true self, and once again take your place in the sun. Celebrate your being present in the world! What were the eleven wonderful qualities and attributes that the fairies gave you at birth? Make a list of them, and pin it somewhere where you can easily see it every morning. Be sure to read it aloud to yourself at least once a day because we learn most easily from the sound of our own voice."

Gateways to a beautiful life

1. The main work of every human being is inner work.
   Each day, do something significant to deepen yourself.

2. See your life as a fantastic growth school. Everything that you experience, both good and challenging, has come to you to teach you the lesson that you most needed to learn at that particular stage of your evolution as a person. Understand the truth and keep asking yourself, "What opportunity does this person or situation represent in terms of your personal growth"? This is a great source of inner peace.

3. Be true to yourself as the best life is the authentic life. Never betray yourself. Take off your social mask and have the personal bravery to present the real you to the world.

4. Remember that we collect what we project. Our outer lives are nothing more than a mirror image of our inner lives. Pour light into your dark side. Become aware of the feeble assumptions, limiting beliefs, and fears that are keeping you small, and your exterior world will change.

5. We see the world not as it is but as we are. Know that the truth in any given circumstance is filtered through your personal stained glass window and your personal context. Clean up the windows and you'll clean up your life. Then you'll see the truth.

6. Believe in your heart: its wisdom never lies. Follow the quiet promptings of your heart and you'll be led in the direction of your destiny.

7. Be curious about your life. In surrendering control, you'll create a space for possibilities to enter and treasures to follow.

8. Care for yourself. Do something each day to nurture your mind, body and spirit. These are essential acts of self-respect and self-love.

9. Build human connections. Dedicate yourself to deepening your bonds with the people around you. Focus on helping others achieve their dreams, and be more concerned with self-less service rather than self-gratification.

10. Leave a legacy. The deepest longing of the human heart is the need to live for a cause greater than oneself.

- The Saint, Surfs & the CEO

Thoughts are Crucial

- As thoughts change, moods, feelings and emotions will follow. So will actions and behaviour.

- Change your thinking and you will also change the way you feel.

- Challenge the beliefs that hold you back or harm you and you will change the way you feel.

- Notice when you are falling into dreary or pessimistic thinking and take positive action and you will change the way you feel.

- Limit the attention you give to what is disappointing or hurtful – and you will change the way you feel.

- Increase the attention you give to what is positive, uplifting, hopeful and supportive – and you will radically change the way you feel.

4 𝒲ays to improve your life

1. **Renew your mind:**

   Everyday cells in your body are being renewed. Make sure you do that with your mind. Renew! Put new thoughts in there.

2. **Replace old mindsets:**

   Often we think all we need to do is adopt a more positive way of thinking. We have to consciously get rid of old mindsets and then start to replace them with new patterns of thinking.

3. **Realign your thinking:**

   By regularly asking yourself "Is this the right way to think?"

4. **Re-establish your convictions.**

Listen to the Buddha

"We are what we think. With our thoughts, we create the world."

Give Yourself Good Advice

Self-respect soars when you know that you can trust your good advice. When you don't know what to do or where to turn to, turn to yourself. Write yourself a letter: "Dear Mary… outlining the situation and offering the wisdom of your own internal wise being." Stepping back mentally to address yourself will give you invaluable perspective and a chance to see familiar situations in a new way. "Feeling silly" is no impediment to making great discourses.

Use these prompts:
- The central issue seems to be…
- What's getting in the way is…
- Change will come when…

Remember:

No one knows you better than you yourself. Value you inner wisdom.

LIFE...

The beauty of life is to give,
The secret of life is to dare,
The opportunity of life is to serve,
The essence of life is to care...

Prayer of
Saint Francis of Assisi

This is a prayer I learned at school. St. Francis (1182-1226)
was the Italian founder of the Franciscan order of monks.

Lord, make me an instrument of your peace.
Where there is hatred, let me sow love;
where there is injury, pardon;
where there is doubt, faith;
where there is despair, hope;
where there is darkness, light;
and where there is sadness, joy.

    O Divine Master, grant that I may not so much seek
    to be consoled as to console;
    to be understood as to understand;
    to be loved as to love.
    For it is in giving that we receive;
    it is in pardoning that we are pardoned;
    and it is in dying that we are born to eternal life.

        - Amen

Values of Success by Edward Carr

Faith
- Faith is to end the day knowing that there will be another day tomorrow.
- Faith is knowing that where I'm going, no matter how hard it will be, I'm going to love it.
- Faith is feeling that when it's wild and unfriendly, you gain the most.
- Faith is knowing that even when everything looks most tangled, giving up is not an option.

Honesty
- Honesty is owning your dreams.

Compassion
- Compassion is realizing a divine harmony with the place you are in.

Loyalty
- Loyalty is holding on no matter how hard it gets.
- Loyalty is crossing a beautiful valley but quickly maintaining your purpose.
- Loyalty is never ceasing to remember why you set out.
- Loyalty is never forgetting your dream even when the way looks impossible.
- Loyalty is being part of any challenge and holding on to what excites you.

Love
- Love is the joy of belonging to each other.
- Love is caring for those around you.
- Love is belonging to each other at every exciting moment.
- Love is being with people you belong to.
- Love is waiting with the door open ready to go and do things together.
- Love endlessly surrounds you with magnificence and life.
- Love is doing things together and enjoying each moment as it happens.

Passion:

eagerness,

excitement,

fervor,

fire,

heat,

intensity,

rapture,

joy,

spirit,

zest,

zeal.

Aspire…

- To be kinder to yourself and other people.

- To 'mind' less if others criticize you.

- To worry less and laugh more.

- To accept as well as give encouragement and appreciation.

- To trust your capacity to be creative.

- To forgive yourself as well as others for past failings and hurts.

- To be able to enjoy your successes.

- To be able to say what you mean.

- To stand up for what your care about.

- To trust and love yourself.

"You have to take the plunge to expose your true self."

- **Jim Carrey**

Wise Words by Tony Ryan in The Ripple Effect

- <u>Believe in your talents:</u> When you believe in your own talents, you can create daily changes all around you. Have you ever wondered why you have been placed on Earth in this life time? Here is one possibility. You are here to live up to your God-given potential, to make the most of whatever talents you were given at birth through your life. Whatever your talent, it is up to you to do the absolute best that you can develop to it. When you do this, the ripples from your actions will naturally be more effective because you will be doing what you are best at doing. However, if you fail to make the most of your talent, you will not only let yourself down, but the many others who would have benefitted from your efforts. Admittedly, it may not always be easy to display your talents freely and openly. Talented people who achieve goals in life do two things well. The first is that they clearly visualize their goals, mentally rehearsing the end result over and over again in their mind. The second is that they persevere with the many tiny steps needed to put the goals into place.

- <u>Create new ideas:</u> A single creative thought can lead to a new product or practice that may eventually change your life, as well as the lives of many other people. The human brain is the most phenomenal entity in the known world. It is one hundred billion neurons dancing to a universal song. It is the creator of your reality at every moment of your life. At one time or another, someone's brain has been responsible for every new idea that has ever been created on our planet. And every time one of these new ideas is released for others, it sets off ripples that change the world forever. If you wish to generate the ripples with your own intellect, then here are a few exercises that may help you to create innovative ideas:

1) Everyday, ask key questions such as "Why and what if?" When you seek answers around you, your thinking is stimulated to consider alternatives. If you neglect to ask these questions, you may be accepting everything just as it is.

2) Consciously exercise your intellect by brainstorming every day. To begin with, you could generate a list of ridiculous and revolutionary ideas on different topics.

- Re-discover your spirit: When you re-discover your spirit for life, your inner energy will create special ripples every day of your life. What would you do if you were visited later tonight by an angel who proceeded to inform you that tomorrow would be the last day of your life?

- Show up: Choose to be present in your life. Experience the fullness of participation rather than giving lack-luster half efforts. Refuse to accept pale imitations of the real thing.

- Pay attention to what has heart and meaning: Do not be swayed by those who feel threatened by the truth and honesty of your emotions. Feel proud of your passion every day.

- Enjoy simple pleasures: Sing a song with gusto, dance in a way that releases your body, become enchanted by stories you hear.

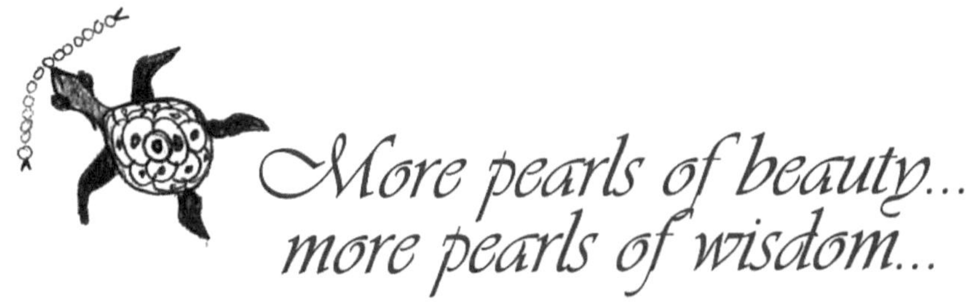

More pearls of beauty...
more pearls of wisdom...

Aren't we so thankful to Bono and Gibran and Santana for sharing these insights for us to learn and internalize? Go on, enjoy and take them to heart!

- Life is full of optical illusions.
  - Grant Frazier

- Ultimately, magic finds you, if you let it.
  - Tony Wheeler

- DANGEROUS IS THE LIE WE TELL OURSELVES.
  - Gabriel Pensador

- Power is nothing unless you can turn it into influence.
  - Condoleezza Rice

- If indeed, you must be candid, be candid beautifully.
  - Kahlil Gibran

- Each person's life is lived as a series of conversations.
  - Deborah Tannen

- The only way to have a life is to commit to it like crazy.
  - Angelina Jolie

- If you want to be successful, just meditate, man. God will tell you what people need.
  - Carlos Santana

- We must be willing to get rid of the life we've planned so as to have the life that is waiting for us.
  - Joseph Campbell

- The moment an individual succumbs to the fear of making a fool of himself, he loses all chances of acting heroically.
  - Miguel De Unamuno

- Whenever you see darkness, there is extraordinary opportunity for the light to burn brighter.
  - Bono

- Leadership is not being nice. It is being right and being strong. To that, one can safely add: it can be warm as the sun and friendly as the rain.
  - Anonymous

- All the devils respect virtue.
  - Ralph Waldo Emerson

- Unpunctuality is a vile habit.
  - Winston Churchill

- Music can change the world.
  - Ludwig Van Beethoven

- Great hopes make great men.
  - Thomas Fuller

- Never take anything for granted.
  - Benjamin Disraeli

- The price of greatness is responsibility.
  - Winston Churchill

- All virtue is summed up in dealing justly.
  - Aristotle

- He that has no patience has nothing at all.
  - Italian Proverb

- ...And will you succeed? Yes! You will, indeed!
  (98 and 3/4 percent guaranteed).
  - Dr. Suess

- My country, right or wrong, but still my country.
  - Stephan Decatur

- The greatest wealth is contentment with a little.
  - English Proverb

- Honesty is the first chapter in the book of wisdom.
  - Thomas Jefferson

- The best way to destroy an enemy is to be a friend.
  - Abraham Lincoln

- As soon as you trust yourself, you will know how to live.
  - Johann Wolfgang Van Goethe

- By far the most important form of attention we can give
  our loved ones is listening.
  - M. Scott Peck

- If you saw yourself as God sees you, you would smile a lot.
  - Anonymous

- Everyone, no matter how poor, can give something. More than
  money, the world needs love and sympathy.
  - J.P. Vaswani

- To make your dreams come true, wake up.
  - Arab Proverb

- To go fast, run alone; to go far, walk together.
  - African Proverb

- If you don't like something, change it; if you can't change it, change the way you think about it.
  - European Proverb

- Be like a duck. Calm on the surface, but always paddling underneath.
  - Michael Caine

- Fear doesn't exist anywhere except in the mind.
  - Dale Carnegie

- Only those who risk going too far can possibly find out how far one can go.
  - T.S. Eliot

- Miracles happen if you believe strongly enough. I'd like to tell people that even if a situation seems hopeless, don't give in. Persevere. If you truly believe, magic will happen. It happened with me.
  - Hritik Roshan

- To some degree, you control your life by controlling your time.
  - Conrad Hilton

When it's Love you are Seeking

* **Take good care of your body:**
  Choose with care what you eat and drink; how you sleep and exercise; how you drive yourself; the care you give to your surroundings. Value your physical existence.

* **Take good care of your mind:**
  Choose what you pay attention to; what you read, watch on TV and think about; how effectively you stimulate, extend, challenge and inspire yourself. Value your intellectual existence.

* **Take good care of your inner world:**
  Allow yourself time for the activities (and non-action) that make you feel good about life, that bring you in touch with your senses; that make you feel in touch and alive; honour what takes you beyond yourself; what inspires and supports you most deeply. Value your spiritual existence.

* **Take good care of your emotions:**
  Recognize your strengths and talents; know what supports you; spend time with people who uplift and encourage you; be good company for yourself; trust your capacity for resilience. Value your emotional existence.

* **Take good care of your part in the social universe:**
  Notice how you affect other people; take seriously your power to influence others positively; to lift their mood, support and encourage them. Value your social existence.

One is not born into the world to do everything but to do something.

- Henry David Thoreau

Power Notes
By Rhonda Byrne

- When you fall in love with life, every limitation disappears. You break limitations on money, health, happiness, and the limits of joys in your relationships. When you fall in love with life, you have no resistance, and whatever you love appears in your life almost instantaneously. Your presence will be felt when you walk into a room. Opportunities will pour into your life, and your slightest touch will dissolve negativity. You will feel better than you thought it was possible to feel. You will be filled with unlimited energy, excitement, and an unquenchable zest for life. You will feel as light as a feather, like you're floating on air, and everything you love will just seem to fall at your feet. Fall in love with life, unleash the power within you, and you will become unlimited and invincible!

- When you are really excited about anything that has happened, and you feel amazing, capture that energy and imagine your dream. Quick flashes of imagining and feeling your dreams are all you need to harness the power of your excited feelings for what you want! This is the joy of creating your life!

- You can harness the power of good feeling to the fullest by turning up its volume. To amplify enthusiasm, revel in the feeling of enthusiasm, milk the feeling for all that you can by feeling it intensely. When you feel passion or excitement, revel in those feelings and intensify them by feeling as deeply as you can. The more you amplify your good feelings, the greater the love you give, and the results you will receive back in your life will be nothing short of spectacular.

- Life isn't happening to you; life is responding to you. Life is your call! Every area of your life is your call. You are the creator of your life. You are the writer of your life story. You are the director of your life movie. You decide what your life will be by what you give out.

- Every day is an opportunity for a new life. Every day you stand at the tipping point of your life. And, on any day you can change the future through the way that you feel.

- The better you feel, the better life gets.

- Amplify your good feelings by thinking about all the things you love. Count the things you love nonstop one after the other. Keep listing everything you love until you start feeling amazed.

- All the things you want are motivated by the good feelings they will give you! And how do you receive the good things in your life? Good feelings! Dollars want you! Health wants you! Fame wants you! Happiness wants you! All the things you love want you! They are bursting to come into your life, but you have to give good feelings to bring them to you. You don't have to battle and struggle to bring them to you. Don't struggle to change the circumstances of your life. Give love through your good feelings and what you want will appear!

- If you find faith wavering, just put a dot in the center of a large circle and next to the dot write the name of your desire. As often as you like, look at your drawing of the dot in the circle, knowing your desire is the size of that dot for the force of love!

- Imagine what you want. Imagine and feel the love of having it. Imagine every scene and situation you can with what you want and feel that you have it now. Try spending seven minutes each day imagining and feeling having what you want. Do it each day until you feel as though you already have your desire. Do it until you know your desire belongs to you, as you know your name belongs to you.

Don't ask why 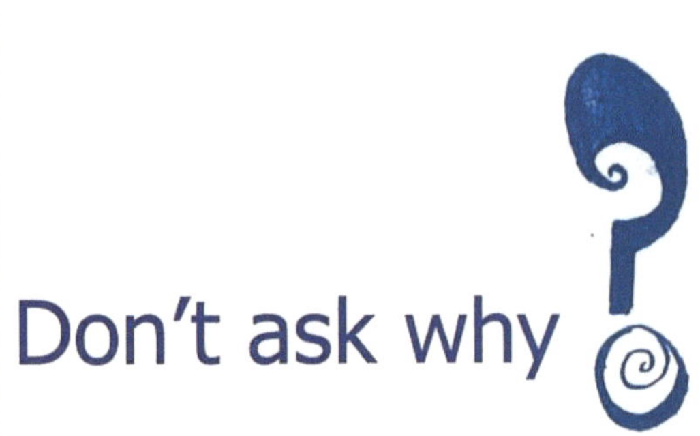

At a stressful moment, or when you feel empty and despairing, do not ask: "Why is this happening to me?". Ask "What can I learn here?", "What will support me to get through this?", " What strengths do I already have from other situations?" and "What's my next step?"

When you are depressed/sad

- **Change your body posture:** Almost inevitably as your thoughts bring you down, your body will reflect this. Moving your body may not solve everything but it will certainly support a more positive, uplifting outlook. Your body reflects your emotions, and sends powerful messages to your mind.

- Shift your thoughts, your attention, away from the causes of your depression, from the justifications for your depression, and from fantasizing about what you need in order for your depression to disappear.

- **Engage with something beyond yourself:** Whatever your activity of choice, let it be as demanding and engaging as possible. Often a change in physical environment will support a significant inner shift.

Intensify your mood

- Sit somewhere beautiful and comfortable. Take in your surroundings. Switch on the right, creative side of your brain by envisaging yourself to be relaxed, open, daring. Enjoy what you see!

Ask :   What's the most outrageously beautiful, original, atypical thing that I've not yet done?
Ask :   What would most magnificently express my love for life and gratitude for my own life ?
Ask :   Whose permission do I need ?

The Six Mistakes of Man

The Roman philosopher and statesman, Cicero wrote this some 2000 years ago; the six mistakes man makes:

1. The delusion that personal gain is made by crushing others.

2. The tendency to worry about things that cannot be changed or corrected.

3. Insisting that a thing is impossible because we cannot accomplish it.

4. Refusing to set aside trivial preferences.

5. Neglecting development and refinement of the mind, and not acquiring the habit of reading and studying.

6. Attempting to compel others to believe and live as we do.

A Sea of Change

You can have a sea of change without
ever leaving home. A positive life is
clear and simple. It means reaching
for the best in yourself, always. And
believing that the best is there to be
found. It also means discovering that
to be at your best does not involve
being better than any other human
being. Not worse, either.

Song of the Open Road

- Walt Whitman

From this hour, freedom!
From this hour I ordain myself loos'd
of limits and imaginary lines,
Going where I list, my own master, total and absolute,
Listening to others, and considering well what they say,
Pausing, searching, receiving, contemplating,
Gently, but with undeniable will, divesting myself
of the holds that would hold me.
I inhale great draughts of space;
The east and the west are mine,
and the north and the south are mine.

I am larger, better than I thought;
I did not know I held so much goodness.

All seems beautiful to me;
I can repeat over to men and women,
You have done such good to me,
I would do the same to you.
I will recruit for myself and you as I go;
I will scatter myself among men and women as I go;
I will toss the new gladness and roughness among them;
Whoever denies me, it shall not trouble me;
Whoever accepts me, he or she shall be blessed,
and shall bless me.

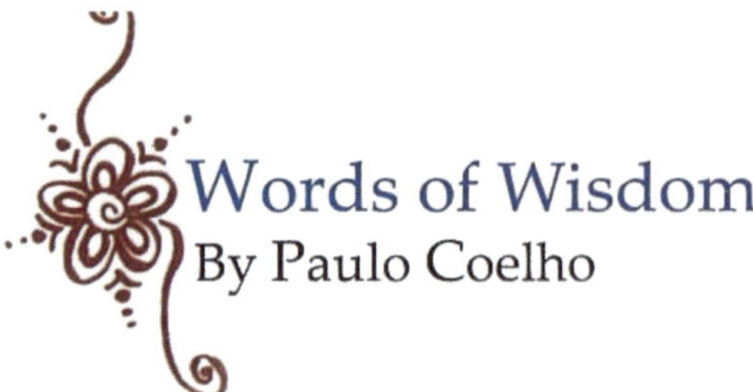

Words of Wisdom
By Paulo Coelho

- Courage! By beginning to journey with that word and continuing with faith in God, you will arrive wherever you need to arrive.

- When everyday seems the same, it is because we have stopped noticing the good things that appear in our lives.

- You have to take risks. We will only understand the miracle of life fully when we allow the unexpected to happen.

- No one can lie, no one can hide anything, when he looks directly into someone's eyes.

- Life is really generous to those who pursue their destiny.

- There is only one way to learn. It's through action.

- Every day God gives us the Sun and also moments in which we have the ability to change everything that makes us unhappy.

- There is only one thing that makes a dream impossible to achieve: the fear of failure.

- When you want something, all the universe conspires in helping you to achieve it.

- The way up to the top of the mountain is always longer than you think. Don't fool yourself, the moment will arrive when what seemed so near is still very far.

- It's the possibility of having a dream come true that makes life interesting.

- What is the real I? It is what you are, not what others make of you.

- I'm totally independent of the good or bad opinion of others.

- I'm beneath no one.

Man-Woman Relationship

- Decide what is worth fighting for.
- Fight lack of respect and having a better way of addressing one another.
- Never threaten.
- If marriage is in threat, let people know.
- Humility is to be fully known.
- Traditions are a lovely way to remember where we come from and where we're going.
- People who take the vow, respect the vow and carry it out.
- Alcohol numbs senses.
- I do not receive because I do not ask.
- Honour love, cherish your vows.
- We can't change our partners but we can change our responses.
- It takes one year to change a relationship.
- Make a request, do not command.
- You are either part of the problem or part of the solution.
- Forgive everyone, let go of the past.
- Forgiveness is the work of the strong. Once you forgive, retributions are given by God.
- He who forgives first, wins.
- Love is giving.
- 5 languages of love
  - Love
  - Time
  - Gifts
  - Acts of Service
  - Words of Affirmation
- Calendar
  - 12 hot nights
  - 3 weekends away
  - 1 holiday a year
  - Once a fortnight date
- Don't argue when you are fatigued.
- Express love to one another.

Pearls...

just pure pearls...
for you...

- Until you spread your wings, you'll have no idea how high you can fly.

- I was taught that the way of progress is neither swift nor easy.

- Fortune favors the brave. All you need is a leap of faith and some spirit. Having a check can change your life.

- Destiny is not a matter of chance but a matter of choice.

- Deeds, not stones, are the true moments of the great.

- Don't be timid and squeamish about your actions. Life is an experiment. The more you experiment, the better.

- To me, the definition of FOCUS is knowing exactly where you want to be today, next week, next month, next year, and then never deviating from your plan. Once you can see, touch and feel your objective, all you have to do is pull back and put all your strength behind your efforts.

When you are inspired by some great purpose, some extraordinary project, all your thoughts break their bonds. Your mind transcends limitations, your consciousness expands in every direction, and you find yourself in a new, great and wonderful world. Dormant forces, faculties and talents become alive, and you discover yourself to be a greater person by far than you ever dreamed yourself to be.
- Patanjali

Light-hearted yet insightful quotations…

- I was born modest, but it didn't last.
  - Mark Twain

- Love is the greatest refreshment in life.
  - Picasso

- What is a weed? A plant whose virtues have
  not been discovered.

- Love is an exploding cigar we willingly smoke.
  - Lynda Barry

- Your imperfections are what make you beautiful.
  - Sandra Bullock

- Art is autobiographical; the pearl is the oyster's
  autobiography.
  - Federico Fellini

- The small courtesies sweeten life, the greater ennoble it.
  - Christian Nestell Bovee

- Art is so wonderfully irrational, exuberantly pointless,
  but necessary all the same.
  - Gunter Gras

- There is one thing both drunks and geographers agree
  upon…. the earth spins round and round.
  - Jose Braga

- Always remember you're unique and so is everyone else.
  - Alison Boulter

A Sure Way to Success

- Having great desire.

- Visualizing in detail exactly what you want.

- Writing your plan to obtain your objectives.

- Taking necessary steps to accomplish your plans.

- Making up your mind so that you are willing to endure the pain of struggle for the comforts, rewards, and the glory that go with achievements.

- Having the right mental attitude, faith and confidence to know that you have the ability to accomplish your goals.

- Putting in necessary work and perseverance to complete your goals.

- Accomplishing and enjoying your goals.

Insights from the book,
'Getting what you want'

by Kare Anderson

- When love is gone, we turn to justice. When justice is gone, we turn to power. When power is gone, we turn to violence.

- Have convictions. Make your choices based on them. Recognize how every choice shapes you and every interaction leaves its mark on you. It is equally important to be good while doing the right thing as it is to actually do the right thing. Look to someone's highest side, especially when disagreeing with them. Remain constant in your loving.

- Once you know that nobody can take from you what is really yours, you stop trying to protect it.

- The only person I control in the entire world is me. People work in their own best interests, not mine.

- If you begin with a loud voice, you soon leave yourself nowhere to go to but to fists.

Live Life
Dr. Shikha Sharma way...

- Eat only fresh food, no fried, junk or leftover food. Exercise three times a week.

- Care about good nutrition. Don't believe in foundation, excessive make-up or bleach. Keep life simple and straight forward. Avoid associating with complicated people and indulging in negative thinking. Get good sleep.

- Do what you believe in. Do not fool yourself. Respect yourself and your abilities. Nurture your mind and body. Do not expect free things from the universe; nor be seduced by the promise of lotteries and easy money. If you are not an improved version of yourself today vis-a-vis yesterday, stop procrastinating and start working on yourself.

- Life is to be lived every moment. Don't fear making mistakes. Fear INACTION.

Why don't you?

- Give a quiet smile to the next person you pass on the street.

- Catch the enthusiasm of a child.

- Pray for someone.

- Write small complimentary notes to your family, and hide them where you know they will find them under their pillows, beside the "biscuit-container" or inside the school bag.

- Say positive things about someone else in their absence.

- Compliment a shop attendant on his excellent service.

- If you see an interesting article, book or news item, send it to someone you know who would appreciate it.

- Buy a tiny gift for a good friend and send it to them with a note that simply says, "Bcoz you deserve it."

- Immediately ask someone to stop if you hear him/her spreading malicious gossip about another person.

- Instead of using your imagination to frighten yourself about the future, put it to use by thinking of ways to remember God is always present.

- Whenever you feel the need to remember that you are a child of God, call friends and acquaintances and ask how they are. Each time we share love with another person through words or a smile, we create a powerful force in the world that combats loneliness.

- On stressful days, tune in to your favourite songs.

- Be kind.

- When you begin to feel disconnected, walk slower, type slower and pay close attention to your work rather than allowing your mind to whirl around.

- Walk barefoot.

- Every night before retiring step outside and reach up to the sky. Thank God and the Universe for this day and for this life.

- Keep a gratitude journal and write down at least five things you can be grateful for at the end of each day.

- Welcome today.

- Read meaningful matters.

- Create a work of beauty.

- Begin again.

  - Slow down.

Modern Quotes

- To send a letter is a good way to go somewhere without moving anything but your heart.

- An enjoyable job is like the fountain of youth.

- People always call it luck when you've acted more sensibly than they have.

- Life isn't science; we make it up as we go long.

- My father used to say if you want to be different, do something different.

- Have a great secret big fat hope for yourself.

- The best present a man can give a woman is his undivided attention.

- When we seek to discover the best in others we somehow bring out the best in ourselves.

- Be thankful for what you have; you'll end up having more.

- One of the nicest things in life is the way we must regularly stop what it is we are doing and devote our attention to eating.

- If you're quiet, you're not living. You need to be noisy and colorful and lively.

- The best of us must sometimes eat our words.

- The first lesson reading teaches is how to be alone.

- Only in grammar can you be more than perfect.

- I never liked anyone who didn't have a temper. If you don't have a temper, you don't have any passion.

- If you do something long enough, it becomes comfortable.

Don't ever quit...

Be true to yourself, it's your journey.

A man with a dream will not be denied.

Don't look back. Yesterday is gone.

Fight the fight of your life. Be a warrior.

Dare to reach out.

Don't let anything bother you, put things behind you.

Throw out your excuses, put your problems behind you.

I will do everything God wants me to.

The only objections that you need to overcome are your own.

All your dreams can come true if you have the courage to pursue them.

I will study and prepare and one day my chance will come.

Effort only fully releases its rewards after the person refuses to quit.

Go confidently in the direction of your dreams. Live the life you have imagined.

Seek out what will inspire you. A life without inspiration is a half-life only.

If you quit, what next?

You have to have a vision of what and when you want in life.

Every Warrior of the Light, has felt afraid of going into battle and

- *has at some time in the past, lied or betrayed someone;*
- *has trodden a path that was not his;*
- *has suffered for the most trivial of reasons;*
- *has at least once, believed he was not a Warrior of the Light;*
- *has failed in his spiritual duties;*
- *has said "Yes," when he wanted to say "No" and*
- *has hurt someone he loved.*

That is why he is a Warrior of the Light, because he has been through all this and yet has never lost hope of being better than he is.

Flowers are the sweetest things
God ever made and forgot to
put a soul into.
- Henry Ward Beecher

Anthony Robbins' Principles for Success

1. Raise your standards:

    - Convert those "shoulds" into "musts" and your
      entire life changes.
    - When you feel that you absolutely must get
      something done, you'll find a way.

2. Change your limiting beliefs. 

3. Model strategies that work.

4. Intensify your emotions:

    - Turn a crushing blow, a setback, or a problem
      into the muscle of life – psychological strength.
      Look at it as a gift of God and find a way to
      use it.

5. Give much more than you expect to receive:

    - If each day you can sincerely feel like you've
      given something of value to those around you,
      I can promise you, you'll experience the ultimate
      richness of life; a life of meaning and joy.

The fire inside you

Inside of you is the fire of life. That fire is your passion, your life purpose, your mission and your fulfilment.

It ignites and burns brightly inside of you when you are doing whatever it takes to live your dreams. When you're fired up, your fire warms others, igniting their flames and creating excitement and a desire to join you so they can make their dreams come true too.

When you're fired up, you feel strong, vibrantly alive and courageous. You believe you can overcome any obstacle and meet any challenge head-on and win. You believe you can achieve what may have seemed unthinkable to you in the past.

You can have more happiness and success than you ever imagined. It all starts inside of you with your fire and your dreams. The choice is always yours. The time to live the life of your dreams is now. As Goethe once said, "Whatever you can do, or dream you can, begin it. Boldness has genius, power and magic in it. Begin it now."

- Anne Whiting

Beautiful words by Oprah Winfrey

- As you become more clear about who you really are, you'll be better able to decide what is best for you – the first time around.

- If you concentrate on what you don't have, you will never, ever have enough.

- Breathe. Let go. And remind yourself that this very moment is the only one you know you have for sure.

- Do the one thing you think you cannot do. Fail at it. Try again. Do better the second time. The only people who never tumble are those who never mount the high wire. This is your moment. Own it.

- Doing the best at this moment puts you in the best place for the next moment.

- Follow your instincts. That's where true wisdom manifests itself.

- For everyone of us that succeeds, it's because there's somebody there to show you the way out.

- I try to take every conflict, every experience, and learn from it. Life is never dull.

- I believe that every single event in life happens through an opportunity to choose love over fear. I don't think of myself as a poor deprived ghetto girl who made good. I think of myself as somebody who from an early age knew I was responsible for myself, and I had to make good.

- I don't think you ever stop giving. I really don't. I think it's an on-going process. And it's not just about being able to write a cheque. It's being able to touch somebody's life.

- I feel that luck is preparation meeting opportunity.

- I have a lot of things to prove to myself. One is that I can live my life fearlessly.

- If you want to accomplish the goals of your life, you have to begin with the spirit.

- Passion is energy. Feel the power that comes from focusing on what excites you.

- Real integrity is doing the right thing, knowing that nobody's going to know whether you did it or not.

- Surround yourself only with people who are going to lift you higher.

- The biggest adventure you can take on is to live the life of your dreams.

- The greatest discovery of all times is that a person can change his future by merely changing his attitude.

- The more you praise and celebrate your life, the more there is in life to celebrate.

- The thing you fear most has no power. Your fear of it is what has the power. Facing the truth will really set you free.

- Think like a queen. A queen is not afraid to fail. Failure is another stepping stone to greatness.

- Turn your wounds into wisdom.

- Understand that the right to choose your own path is a sacred privilege. Use it. Dwell on the possibility.

- Unless you choose to do great things with it, it makes no difference how much you are rewarded, or how much power you have.

- What God intended for you goes far beyond anything you can imagine.

- What I know is that, if you do work that you love, and the work fulfills you, the rest will come.

- When I look into the future, it's so bright it burns my eyes.

- Where there is no struggle, there is no strength.

- *The policy of being too cautious is the greatest risk of all.*
  - *Jawaharlal Nehru*

- *God doesn't require us to succeed; He only requires that we try.*
  - *Mother Teresa*

- *No legacy is so rich as honesty.*
  - *Willam Shakespeare*

- *Never discourage anyone who continually makes progress, no matter how slow.*
  - *Plato*

- *Risk! Risk anything! Care no more for the opinion of others, for those voices. Do the hardest thing on earth for you. Act for yourself. Face the truth.*
  - *Katherine Mansfield*

- *He who walketh with wise men shall be wise.*
  - *The Bible*

- Stand above petty praise and
  blame of the world.
  - Swami Ramdas

- Experience is what you get when
  you don't get what you want.
  - Dan Stanford

- People will forget what you said,
  people will forget what you did, but
  people will never forget how you
  made them feel.
  - Maya Angelou

- Like timidity, bravery is also
  contagious.
  - Munshi Premchand

- You will never "find" time for anything.
  If you want time, you must make it.
  - Charles Buxton

- He who is overcautious, will accomplish little.
  - Schiller

- Our deeds, good or evil, follow us like shadows.
  - Buddha

- No great man ever complains of want of
  opportunity.
  - Ralph Waldo Emerson

- I always entertain great hopes.
  - Robert Frost

- Genius is nothing but a greater
  aptitude for patience.
  - Buffon

- Expect victory and you make victory.
  - Dr. Preston Bradley

- Enthusiasm is the greatest asset in the
  world. It beats money and power and
  influence.
  - Henry Chester

- Where there is no vision, people perish.
  - Proverbs 29:18

- The best prize life offers is the chance to
  work hard at work worth doing.
  - Theodore Roosevelt

- When love and skill work together, expect a
  masterpiece.
  - Charles Reale

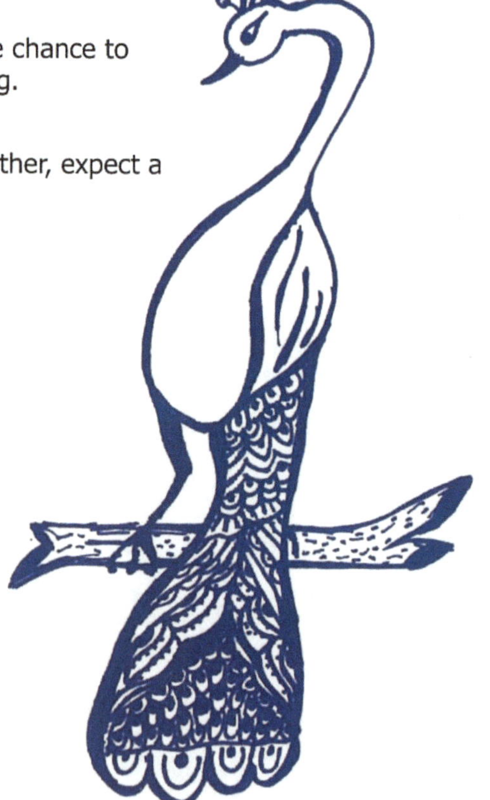

"Difficult Times"

Difficult times simply mean the experience of an unconscious confused mind – your thinking is stuck. Becoming aware of how the mind works, the role of thinking, the value of feelings and an awareness of your source of wisdom is the way out. Any life situation or event can be the catalyst or trigger for a confused mind. Counseling (i.e, listening, questioning or teaching enable you to see for yourself how you create your reality together with an awareness of your source of wisdom) can help you move beyond a stuck mind and provide you with the awareness to do so any time.

"Sometimes great ideas are born of desperation"

Final Words....

I hope you enjoyed the beautiful words. Life is too beautiful to sit back and complain. Go and grab life with your hands. With God, everything is possible. Life is not a destination but a beautiful journey. Believe in the best and trust God. Make lots of noise, listen to loud music, smile and laugh a lot, enjoy being loved and loving. Be grateful for all your gifts in life. Enjoy each and every day of your life! My friends, la vie en rose.

Moheindu Chemjong is a humanitarian worker with postgraduate degrees in management (MBA) and political science. Moheindu enjoys reading, writing, painting, playing and listening to world music.

She believes in living each day as it comes as every day is a gift from God to see, learn, enjoy and do something completely new. Colours, voices, words and various art forms mesmerize her.

A global citizen fascinated by the simplicity of her fellow countrymen, no matter which country she travels to or works or lives in, her heart belongs to her motherland and her people.

Wisdom Pearls
by Moheindu Chemjong

ISBN 978-9937-2-7372-5

9 789937 273725 >

www.ingramcontent.com/pod-product-compliance
Lightning Source LLC
Chambersburg PA
CBHW041601110726
48005CB00002B/245